Lately, I've been alo

by
William

Lately, I've been drinking alone.

by William Bortz
copyright 2014 William Bortz
author photo by Michelle Esquivel
back cover edits by Chelsie Ver Steeg

To my dear friend, Anthony.
"Don't limit your thoughts to words."

Table of Contents

Soak

it is not like it was just yesterday
that you got less interested and
we stopped talking
it has been two years
but I think I am still in the process
of recovering
I am beginning to notice
those not so ugly things
like how on a hot summer day
when it rains
the water brings out the dirty smell
of the freshly laid pavement
and the cigarette smoke
barreling out between my teeth
looks like a tidal wave
heading to shore
ready to swallow it whole
I think about very little
not about god
or about love
I do not lay awake at night
I sleep, but not well
I get mad at the construction
and the fog that impedes
on my morning drive to work
I am always late
always in a hurry
I guess the process of recovery
is longer than what I was told
it would be as a child
like I was stabbed
and no matter how many
napkins I find

I cannot soak up the whole mess
at once

June

this month
I will teach myself
to only let those
who have the kind
of hands that
plant flowers,
and not those that
uproot them,
burrow beneath
my skin

but, alas

medication decides my moods
and yet they tell me
to believe that tomorrow is
as reasonable as I am

beauty

how sick are we
to curse the sun
when it burns our skin
and to curse
the seas
when they choke us up
when all we want
is to feel something
or feel whole

in caring:

I met a girl
in the bar
who only drank
clear liquor
and she laughed
at all my jokes
and twirled her
hair around those
skinny fingers
of hers
we were drunk
but only slightly
she asked me where
I was spending the night
but smiled like
she already knew
we had sex in
her bed even though
I have never dreamt
in it before
and did not know
her name or even
her favorite color
only that she
liked to sleep on
silk sheets and
had a few pictures
of James Dean
hanging on the wall
by morning I called her
pretty and knew her
favorite color was red
that was the color
of the lipstick that

stained my neck
and she didn't look
beautiful when she
slept or even cute
she only looked like
a stranger, or someone
I hardly knew
and I felt like
an intruder
so I left and
tried not to imagine
us being in love
or remembering
the freckles
on her legs
after she
eventually left me
I walked down the
stairs and out into
the street where
everything was thoughtless
and dirty just
like I am
and didn't feel a
thing, because
what is white will
become blackened
and who we love
will eventually die
or follow their dreams
to some place better
so what is
really the point
in caring to
remember

a hope, a prayer. please god don't leave me again

I will catch the next bus
to your side of town
if you brew up a pot of coffee
I will knock twice real quiet
if you promise to answer quickly
I will tell you every single itch
I have felt on my skin
over the past two years
if you will listen intently
and follow up with a kiss
I will ask about your mother
if you tell me that she is better
and tending to her garden again
I will help you with the dishes
if I can dry my hands in your hair
I won't ask you what happened last summer
if you tell me all your future plans
and if you are unsure, lost, or have none
I promise not to question you
if you can tell me why
I write your name in each day's lonely sky
I will tell you how it looks different every time
if you tell me to stay
when the sun comes up
I promise not to say a word
I won't even make a sound

starlight

I find myself going back
to that night so often
how the stars laughed at me
because they were
anything but lonely
the way the moon
hung so high above me
comparing its fullness
to my emptiness
even the road had
more company than I
the only bed that could
produce the dreams I
so desperately needed
was the last one I would
lay my head down on
thinking back at that
night, the yellow lines
stretching into the blackness
headed for infinity
or some other
place I did not belong
I should have
closed my eyes
gripped the wheel as
tightly as I could muster
and swerved with all
the strength I
had left in me

monsters

my dreams are
making you
a monster
someone I have
come to fear
to hide from
to repress

in growing:

people are always saying
to leave the parts of you
that have died
in the past

yet I look back
wondering how I
ended up
being too weak
to forget

echoes

I visit the sea
to hear the sounds
of my ribcage
to feel the echoes
of your voice
bouncing off the walls
of the place
you once called
home

help

I won't ask you for help
because by doing that I am
admitting that I am not
all together right now

10;

the other night
I dreamt that I died
the first thing I did
after waking up
in a panic
was feel my skin
to make sure
it was still in tact
this morning when you told me
you didn't love me
like you once did
I just fell to the ground
scared and lost
because there was nothing
I could touch to trick myself
into believing
that I was still whole

selfish

it was so selfish
for me to think
of my hands as tools
that could possibly
fix you
when you said you
were broken
or when you told me
you didn't need love
and I believed
you meant the opposite
and so I told you
that I was
on top of it
and those expectations
you had
I could exceed
it was so selfish
for me to think
that you needed me

12

i'm running out of ways
to compare my heartache
to angry seas
or my emptiness
to the stars in the sky
i am trying to find
the beauty in your absence
but there is none
you are gone
and everything
has turned to shit

3pm

the way your name
grew on me;
the way it fluttered
off my tongue
changed everything
which is why
I no longer
take the long, scenic
way home anymore

Sundays

I don't know a lot about god
but I know that on a warm day
rain feels like heaven
and I don't know a lot about sin
but I know that I felt something
when I pulled off your shirt
and breathed you in
I've never imagined selling
my soul to the devil
but I think I came close when
you asked how long my parents
would be gone, and in those
twenty minutes I didn't
even try to be gentle
I never thought to question
why my mom decided to sleep
with death instead of tucking me in
I have been far too busy finding
the difference between what my pastor
taught me about sex and what
you teach me about religion

something that hopefully gets forgotten

we were drunk
the night was wasted
and the way you said
'I love you'
sounded more like
goodbye

wildfire

my flame flickers
in the darkness, in the black
in the silence
in the sweet stride
of my enemies coming
for me, and it gets buried
in the smoke of their torches
how much energy it must take
to be a wildfire
to be not afraid

forgetting you feels so fucking good.

in forgiveness:

at some point I
stopped being angry
at you
for the way you left
how you were there
for so long
and gone in an instant
our whole relationship
I told you to do things
for yourself before me
or anybody else
and that is what you did
you didn't leave for me
you left for yourself
and although the taste
you left on my lips
is bitter now
I do hope if mine
is still lingering on yours
its stay is short
and sweet

hands

I am dreaming of
your body tangled
with mine
your words trying hard
to find grace
as they fall
out of your mouth
but your hands
my god
your hands
speaking ever so fluently

old bridges

I want to walk
on old bridges
fearing the structure will fail
so I can relive the moment
my bones caved in
when I heard
that first buzz of summer
and the flowers
adored you so much
they bloomed more violently
when entangled
in your hair

atmosphere

your face is the night sky
I look at it in wonderment
how I get lost in it
I wish on every freckle
little stars
lighting up the dark
how I want to kiss them
I stay up late
wishing I could
taste your
atmosphere

second hand smoke

the sweet taste
of morning air
does not even compare
to the second hand smoke
breathed out from
your lungs
and down my throat

infinity

when we die
let's get buried by each other
so we can stretch
out past our coffins
like the roots of trees
displacing the sidewalk
in front of someone's house
and trip them up
like we did on our morning walks
when we were more
than skin and bones
and held hands the
whole way home
let's count the seconds
between our smallest breaths
until one of us
reaches infinity
I want people
to still envy us
after we are
no longer living.
fuck.

relish

the wine is sweeter
the moon burns quieter
my skin is screaming
everything you love
blooms fuller than
the rest

not today

i am not ready
to let the small things
start killing me
again

daydreams

I spend most afternoons
daydreaming of your head
nestled in the curve of my neck
for the same reason
people put so much effort in capturing
lightning in a photograph
I want to be humbled
by the loudest thing in
my world falling silent
if even for just a second

grey

the way you speak of love
makes it sound a lot
like silence

in changing:

nervously, your hands were fumbling
but still felt like feathers on my cheek
and the words you spoke were tired
trying so hard to get some rest
in a cascading wave of limbs
and breaths they weren't satisfied
with my chest
what was once so damn easy
is tired, worn out, and hurts
just as I do

intentions

I have no
intentions
of dismantling
you, but I
cannot stop
you from
pulling yourself
apart

autumn

how many times
do you need
to fall over from
leaning on people
with broken bones
before you realize
you are strong enough
to stand on your own

rivers

there are hundreds
of little rivers
beneath your skin
and I want to
drown myself in
every one of them

a pale yellowish-green flame

she is slowly
filling my lungs
with her breath
cigarette smoke
and dreams of
scarlet evenings
tasting heavily
of love

~

love me politely,
count me gently into your i n f i n i t y

13

I know I love her
because every time
she exhales I become
frantic; deeply worried
that any breath
could be her last

a process

I thought of you leaving me today
and I bit my lip
I decided I should start
easing my way
into the pain of your departure

you aren't a lesson

they say you get that one
who will show you
what loss truly is
but I have met loss
I have spent nights
with it cradling my
sleepless body
I have tasted it on
the lip of a clear glass
I have made love with it
in a downtown studio apartment
I have carved it into every
bathroom stall I spent
the night praying in
please don't be a lesson
I have already learned once before
and am still trying to recover from

after years

everyday is like the first
one I spent with her
frantic, & wondering when
I will find the perfect
moment to kiss her;
smiling like a fool
because I know she
will kiss me back
when I do
find the nerve

seashells

she digs beneath my skin
through the tormented currents
and many swarms of ferocious predators
that are hiding in the depths
yes, I call it love
because even on days
when I am spilling over
and all my demons rush to the surface
she still reaches in without a second thought
just to find seashells

where do the lonely lovers sleep?

oh god
I am scared
I looked at her today
held her gaze
and felt myself welling up
confused, I looked away
never has such a feeling
moved over my bones
in such a tremendous way
after she left
I remained sprawled out
on my back
my right hand tracing
the warmth her skin
had left on my bed
I thought of her eyelashes
I pictured them as butterflies
in a crowded forest
swarming around the trunk of a tree
fluttering; hiding the lively, brown bark
she blinks and they migrate
I follow
hours are gone and it is dark
her side is cold now
and I want to hear her voice
or see her eyes looking up at me
fuck
my chest is cold
where she kept her head
my hands are cold
where I kept hers
I am thinking about
the way that she walks
and how I want to

capture it in pictures
also how I need a recording of her cursing
an angel being vile feels so much like purgatory
that curl in her lips
that hiss in her breath as she sleeps
I need it all
I need to capture it in a tank
so in times like these I can inhale it all
like my last breath of air
god
her fingers and their lines
the creases and indents
I don't know if I want to
keep my distance so I can watch
them open and close like fly traps
or use them to stir my morning coffee
she tastes like what the ocean looks like
just
so vast
so blue
honest with careless thoughts
I look at her and know
that there is not one grain of salt
underneath her changing tides
my fingers get tangled
around a piece of her hair
that got detached from her
beautiful little head
it pulls tightly against my skin
and I need it
I only wish it was her teeth
I may be too honest
and far too overwhelming
but I am fucking scared
because it is now morning
and I love her

1:12am 6/18/14

she is asleep right now
her head resting on my shoulder
and I am thinking about morning
and how far away it is
and how happy I am about that
and how badly I want to kiss her awake
but she is such a tender sleeping body
that I don't dare to even take a deep breath
as to stir her
I will lie awake
staring at the ceiling
until the morning light fades in
feeling completely exhausted
from falling in love
with the tiredness buried
inside of my bones

anxiety

maybe I am unable
to appreciate things
but
I have a hard time
telling the difference
between the stress
of wanting things to
be better
and the anxiety
of trying to hold
them together
when they are

acknowledgements

many thanks to Anthony for being a constant inspiration.
thanks to Adam for great conversation.
thanks to Kalie, Joddi, and Jeremy for always being there.
thanks to my brothers and sisters.
thanks to Chelsie for all the help in putting this together.
special thanks to everyone in between.

end notes

william bortz

author and poet from the Midwest.
thank you for reading, and more so, for existing.

redandhazel.tumblr.com
@BNwillbortz

other books:
'These Ties'
'Petrichor'
'Noema'

67201308R00034

Made in the USA
Lexington, KY
04 September 2017